MILAN IN 3 DAYS

2024

A perfect exploring plan on how to enjoy 3 days in Italy, itinerary, Google map, food guide, shopping, and many local secrets to save time and money.

Clara R. Burgher

All rights reserved. No part of this publication may be reproduced, distributed, or transmitted in any form or by any means, including photocopying, recording, or other electronic or mechanical methods, without the prior written permission of the publisher, except in the case of brief quotations embodied in critical reviews and certain other noncommercial uses permitted by copyright law. Copyright © Clara R. Burgher 2024.

TABLE OF CONTENTS

INTRODUCION

My top tips to save time visiting Milan's must-see attractions

One Last Tip for the Perfect 3-Day Stay in Milan

Visiting Milan in Three Days: The Best Itinerary

Milan Itinerary: Day One - The Historic Center

Day 1 visits

What should I do and see on my second day in Milan?

Visits on day 2

Third day in Milan: Places to Visit

Day 3 visits

Where To Stay In Milan

Visiting Milan in three days with family

BONUS

Travel Journal

INTRODUCION

Do You intend to spend three days in Milan and want to know what to do?

I've prepared a 3-day itinerary in Milan to assist you organize your visit.

During your journey, you will experience all of the city's must-see sights, such as Milan Cathedral, Sforza Castle, and the Navigli district.

In addition to the greatest sites to visit and activities for each step of your plan, I'll provide you with all of my best insights and lodging recommendations based on your budget.

So, what are the greatest locations to see in Milan in three days? Where can I stay?

Let us find out!

My top tips to save time visiting Milan's must-see attractions

When I think of Milan, I always imagine the famed cathedral with its distinctive facade. As a result, it is a definite must-see during your three-day stay in Milan!

Unfortunately, you will not be the only one having this thought at the same moment.

The wait at the Duomo, like the Colosseum in Rome or Westminster Abbey in London, extends across the Square for tens, if not hundreds, of meters each day. It might take many hours to access the city's iconic monuments!

However, there are numerous really easy methods to save time on your three-day vacation to Milan.

I'll go over the three greatest strategies for avoiding queues in detail below!

1. The Milan Pass

The first way to make the most of your three-day vacation to Milan is to get the Milan Pass.

Today, most major tourist destinations offer this sort of City Pass, which is not only very handy for skipping lines at the most popular attractions, but also provides significant discounts.

The Milan Pass is valid for 48 or 72 hours from the first usage, whether for a visit or transportation.

When you book, you will get an email with a printout or a voucher on your smartphone to exchange for the card at the Milan Visitor Centre. It is situated on Via Cusani, just across from the Sforza Castle entrance.

This Pass is the most complete option for touring Milan in three days.

The Milan Pass includes all of the following:
- Skip-the-line ticket to Milan Cathedral (Duomo) includes access to the terraces.
- Free access to Scala Museum and Theater, Brera Picture Gallery, and Museum of Science and Technology.
- A book of discounts for pubs, restaurants, and select guided excursions in Milan lasting more than 72 hours
- A city map

With the purchase of the Milan Pass, you will additionally receive:
- A ticket for the City Sightseeing bus that enables you to jump on and off whenever you want to visit the major attractions
- A free ticket to use public transportation (metro, tram, and bus).

Very convenient if you're weary of walking or if you're visiting Milan with little children.

Visit tiquets.com to get your Milan city pass now.

(Ticket Name: Milan City Pass Zani Viaggi: Admission to 10+ Attractions + public transport.

2. The Milan Digital Pass

The Milan Digital Pass is another alternative for exploring Milan on foot in three days or via public transportation.

It operates on the same concept as the Milan Pass, providing free or reduced-cost entrance to major tourist destinations. The benefit is that you will get your card by email or app download.

The Milan city card covers all of the following services:
- Skip-the-line ticket to Milan's must-see attraction: the Duomo (+ access to the museum and the roof)
- Fast-track access to the Leonardo da Vinci Museum of Science and Technology
- Access to the Ambrosian Picture Gallery.
- The audio guide
- Discount of 10% on another Milan activity.

To acquire your Milan Digital Pass, just visit tiquets.com.

(Ticket Name: Milan City Card: Attractions and Discounts)

3. Skip-the-Line Tickets for Milan Tourist Attractions

The third option for speedy access to all of the key attractions is to acquire skip-the-line tickets for each monument or museum on your three-day agenda in Milan. There are numerous options for both must-see sights and things to do in Milan throughout these three days.

I've provided a few examples here, but you'll see them throughout the book.

To book them, it's once again incredibly easy; simply visit the website:

Visit Milan in 3 Days: The Essentials

- Milan Cathedral (Duomo) @getyourguide.com (Ticket Name: Cathedral and Duomo's Terraces Entrance Ticket)

- La Scala Opera House @tiqets.com(Ticket name: Tickets for La Scala: Guided Tour of the Theater + Museum)

- Sforza Castle@Tiqets.com(Ticket name: Tickets for La Scala: Guided Tour of the Theater + Museum)

- Leonardo da Vinci's The Last Supper at Tiqets.com.(Ticket Name: The Last Supper Tickets)

- Leonardo da Vinci National Museum of Science and Technology @tiqets.com(Ticket name: National Museum Science and Technology Leonardo da Vinci: Entry Ticket)

- Navigli District Cruise@Tiqets.com (Ticket name: Milan Cruises).

- Brera Picture Gallery@Tiqets.com(Tickets for Pinacoteca Ambrosiana)

- Hop-On, Hop-Off Sightseeing Bus@getyourguide.com(Ticket name: 24-, 48-, or 72-Hour Hop-On Hop-Off Bus Ticket)

- San Siro Stadium@tiqets.com. (Ticket name-Ticket for San Siro Stadium Tour: Reserved Entrance)

One Last Tip for the Perfect 3-Day Stay in Milan

If you already have your trip dates (or will have them shortly), you should reserve your accommodations.

Because Milan is one of the most visited cities in the world, the hotels that provide the greatest value for money are sometimes booked months in advance.

As a seasoned traveler, I can promise you that I always find the finest hotel or apartment discounts by arranging ahead of time.

You think that it would be a shame to spoil your trip to Milan by staying in a bad hotel that costs you a lot, right?

So your best chance is to spend 5 minutes now to check out travelers' favorite hotels in Milan. @booking.com

And if you like any of the hotels you discover, book it!

It's quick and simple, and most hotels provide free cancellation. That is the greatest approach to avoid the annoyance of being stuck with just unsatisfactory lodgings at expensive costs.

After you've secured your ideal stay, it's time to continue reading this guide!

Visiting Milan in Three Days: The Best Itinerary

Let us immediately begin your three-day schedule in Milan!

For each day, I'll provide you with all of the information you need to arrange your trips and help you visualize the schedule.

I'm assuming you'll be in Milan for three full days and plan to use the Milan Pass, Milan Digital Pass, or skip-the-line tickets. It's the most efficient method to save time and money throughout your visit!

So, how does one visit Milan in three days?

Milan Itinerary: Day One - The Historic Center

Day 1 visits

- A. the Milan Cathedral (Duomo).
- B. Galleria Vittorio Emanuele II
- C. La Scala Opera House.
- D. Sforza Castle.

- E. Sempione Park
- F. Chinatown.

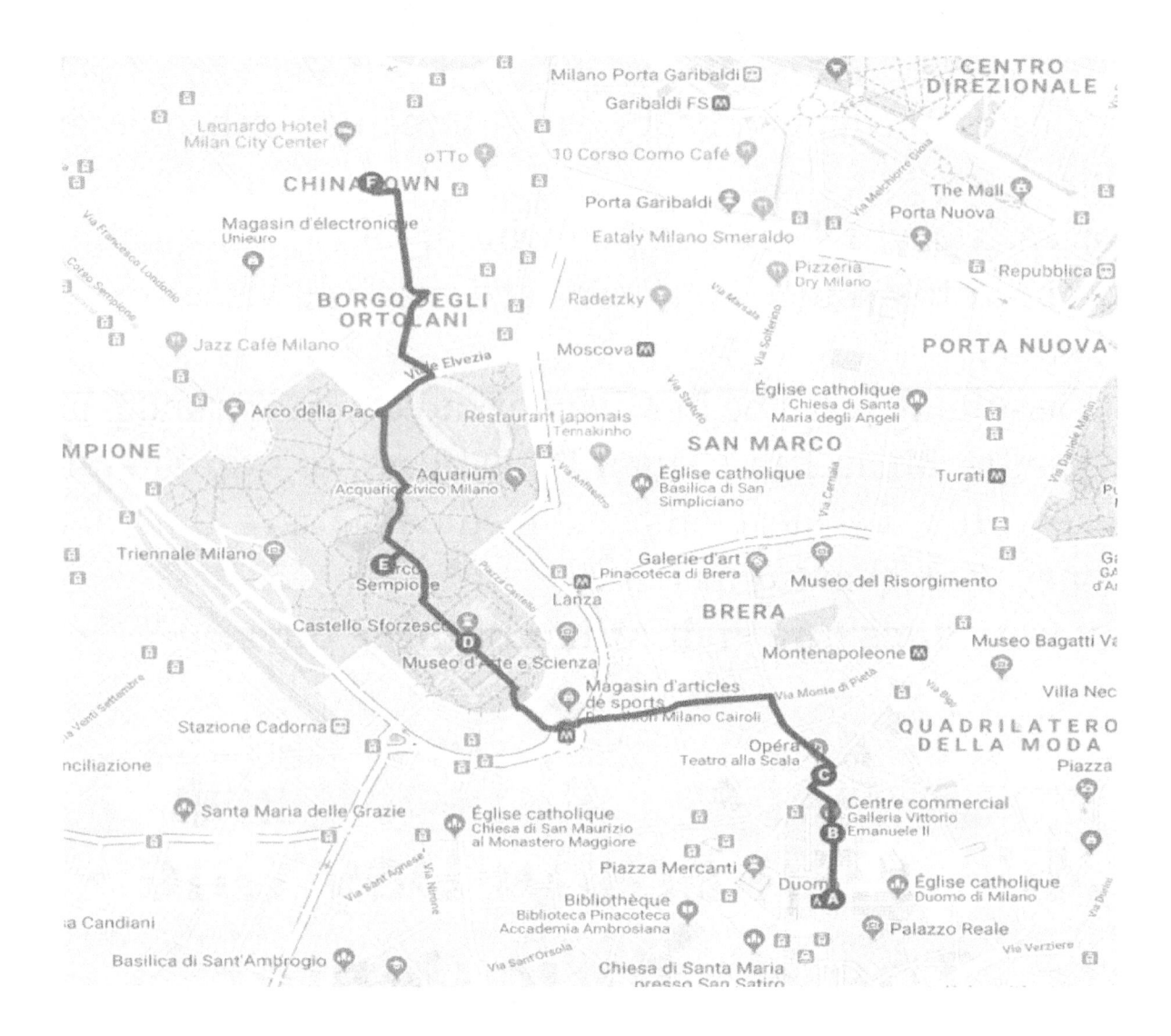

A. Milan Cathedral (Il Duomo)

Il Duomo, often known as Milan Cathedral, is the city's most well-known and important architecture. That's why I recommend that you begin your three-day journey to Milan here.

If you've decided to stay in the historic district, you can simply get there by foot. Otherwise, take the subway (Duomo station) and exit at Piazza del Duomo.

The Duomo is not just the city's greatest attraction, but the world's third biggest cathedral. Construction started in the 14th century and lasted over 500 years. The end product is a spectacular monument that sits in the heart of Milan on Piazza del Duomo, drawing millions of people annually!

To enter the cathedral, you typically have to wait in line for many hours. Book the Milan Pass, Milan Digital Pass, or Skip-the-Line Duomo Cathedral Tour to save time on your visit.

Booking a guided tour (in French) allows you to access without waiting in line:

Before entering the Duomo, take at the 2000 marble sculptures and the 136 spires that proudly point to the sky, giving the cathedral the nickname "marble hedgehog".

Inside, you will see archbishops' naves, sarcophagi, and tombs, as well as a crucifix by Leonardo da Vinci.

You will also be able to visit the Duomo's terrace (by stairs or elevator) for an incomparable perspective of the whole city.

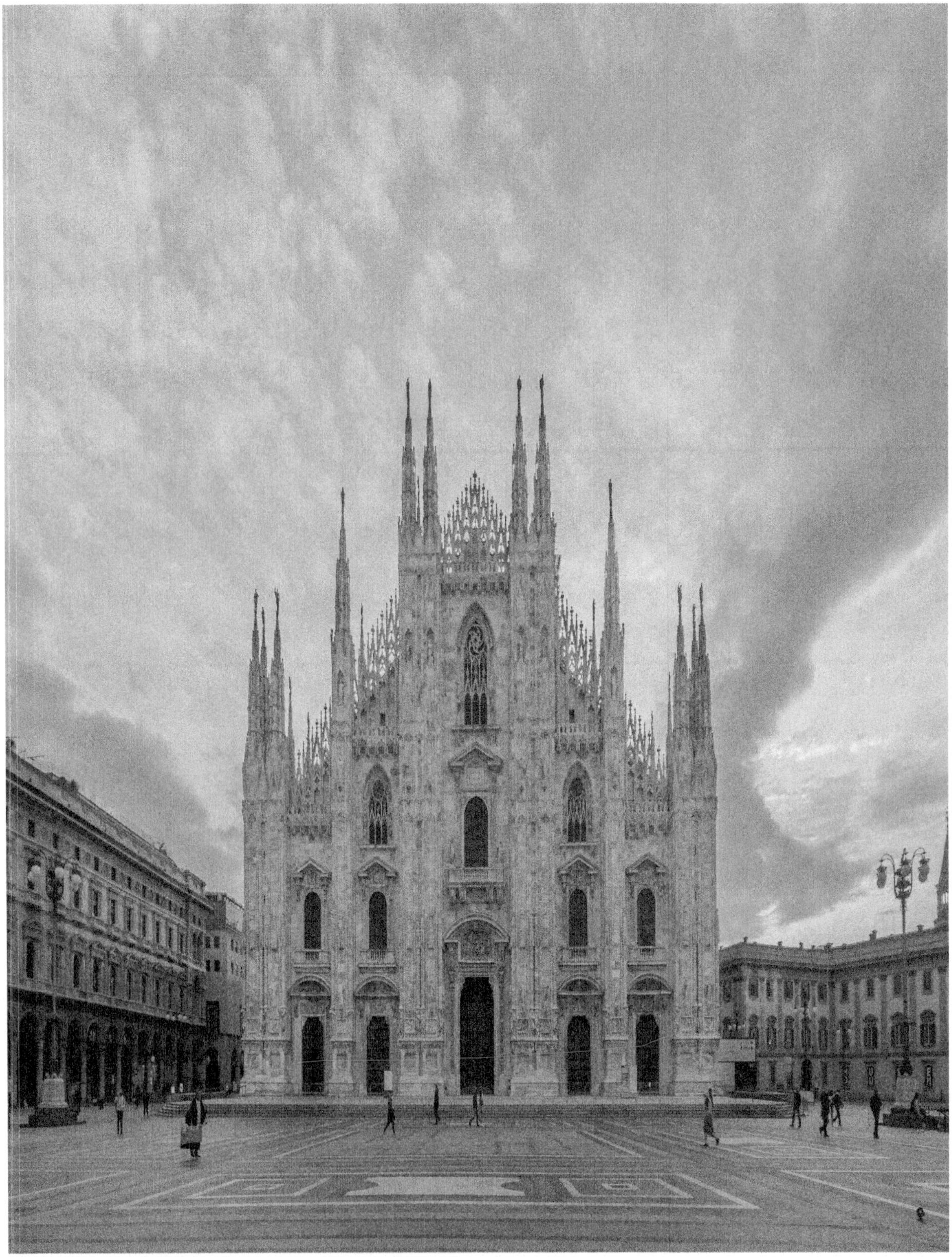

B. Galleria Vittorio Emanuele II

Continue your three-day Milan itinerary by visiting Galleria Vittorio Emanuele II, which is accessible from Piazza del Duomo, to the right as you depart the cathedral.

This luxury arcade, distinguished by its arcades and spectacular glass and iron dome, is home to a variety of high-end stores and eateries.

Even if shopping isn't in your budget, you should still come to see the architecture.

It is regarded as one of Europe's most magnificent buildings, thanks to its neoclassical architecture and baroque inspiration!

C. La Scala

La Scala, situated only a 5-minute walk from the Galleria Vittorio Emanuele, is another must-see Milan landmark.

Exit via the north corridor and cross the little Piazza della Scala, paying special attention to the statue of Leonardo da Vinci in the center. Continue straight for a few meters until you reach La Scala, the historic building that houses the Milan Opera House.

La Scala is among Italy's most prestigious venues. Verdi's classic "Otello" has been played here. This venue has also hosted performances by soprano Maria Callas.

The monument's outer façade may seem unremarkable, yet the inside of the opera theater is luxurious. The museum on the building's left side is also worth visiting since it has a stunning collection of musical instruments and opera costumes.

The opera is only accessible with a guide, and tickets may be ordered directly@tiqets.com.

The MilanPass includes access as well.

If you're a music lover and want to attend an opera, ballet, or concert, you can obtain your tickets at www.teatroallascala.org/en/index.html.

D. Sforza Castle

Next, visit Sforza Castle (also known as Castello Sforzesco).

It is about 1 kilometer from La Scala, so you can simply walk there.

The castle, which was built in the 14th century to safeguard the city from its then-enemy Venice, is also known for housing Leonardo da Vinci's workshops during the Renaissance.

Today, the castle's chambers are home to many museums.
- Museum of Ancient Art
- The Museum of Prehistory
- The Museum Of Decorative Arts
- The Egyptian museum
- The picture gallery
- The museum of musical instruments
- Museum of Furniture

visit tiqets.com to reserve your ticket to see Sforza Castle + audio guide. (Ticket name: Sforza Castle Entry ticket with digital audioguide.

Even if you don't want to visit the museums, you can take a walk across the expansive courtyard, which often holds cultural activities. There is no cost to enter the courtyard.

Crossing it will take you right to Sempione Park, the next destination on your three-day Milan itinerary.

E. Sempione Park

Sempione Park is the city's main park, situated behind the castle.

While strolling in the park, don't miss the opportunity to view

Triennale in the Southwest: a modest museum emphasizing Italian arts and architecture

Arena Civica in the Northeast: a stadium that hosts athletics competitions.

Arco della Pace in the Northwest: Milan's triumphant arch.

If you're visiting Milan with your kids, you may take them to the aquarium, which is also situated in Sempione Park.

F. Milan Chinatown

To conclude your first day in Milan, I recommend seeing the city's Chinatown, which is situated north of the Arco della Pace and is just a 10-minute walk away.

Expect a smaller Chinatown than in New York or Montreal. However, it is an excellent alternative for a fun evening out, where you may find low-cost stores and authentic Asian products.

What should I do and see on my second day in Milan?

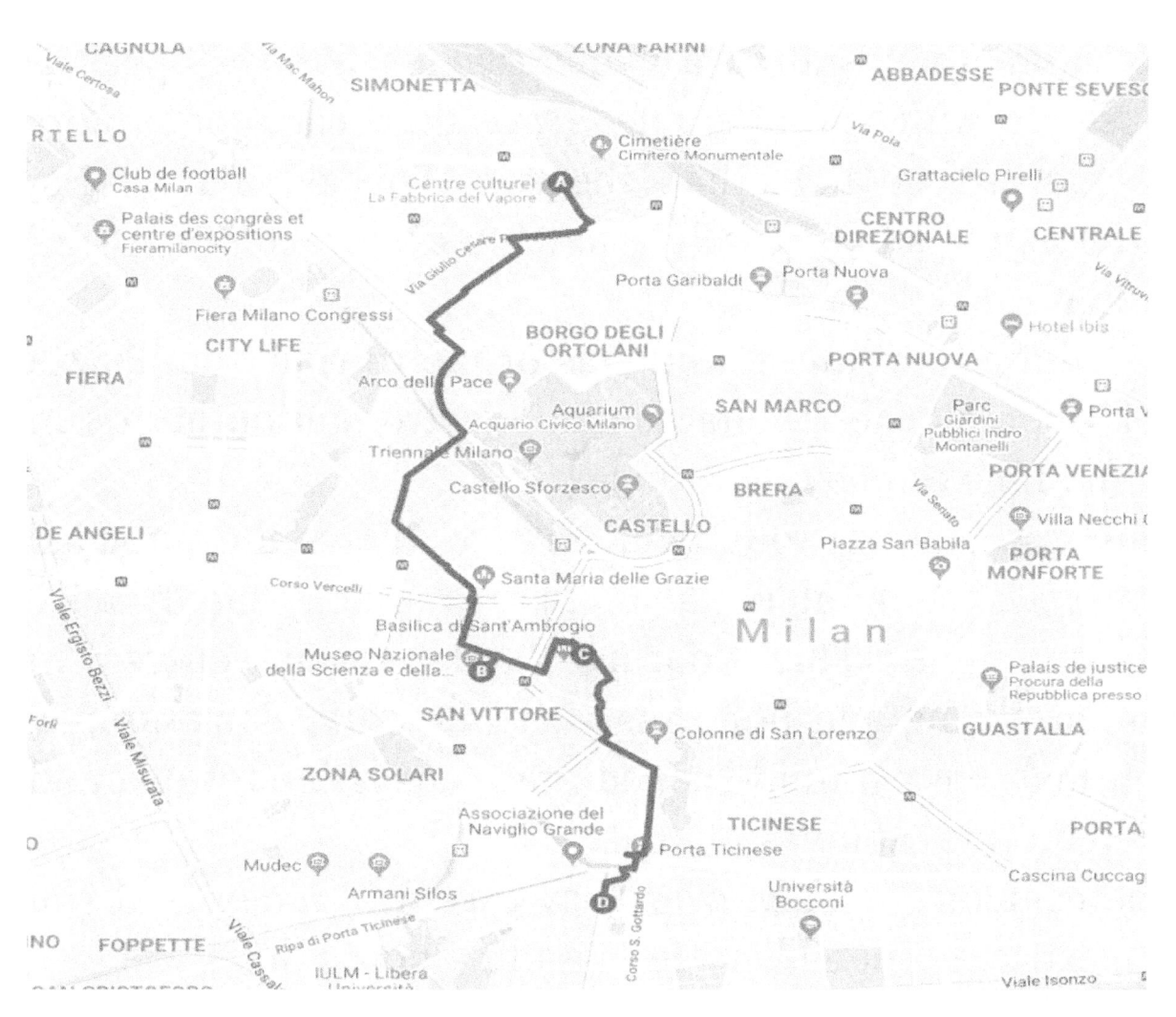

Visits on day 2

- A. Monumental Cemetery
- B. Leonardo da Vinci Museum of Science and Technology.
- C. The Basilica of Sant'Ambrogio
- D. Navigli district

A. Monumental Cemetery

For the second day of your three-day journey to Milan, I recommend visiting the Monumental Cemetery, which is a fascinating place to start the day.

It's more than simply a cemetery; it's a huge open-air museum with innumerable gravesites, each one more unique and creative than the last. This popular tourist attraction is situated only a few hundred meters north of Chinatown.

It's within a twenty-minute bus or metro ride from Piazza del Duomo. The "Monumentale" metro station is just in front of the cemetery entrance.

This fascinating tour will take you to the unusual gravesites of notable Italian figures, whose family have shown remarkable daring and inventiveness in immortalizing and honoring their memory. For example, you may see pyramid-shaped graves, pristine towers, and even marble canopies.

The cemetery is open every day except Monday, and you can expect to spend between 1 and 1.5 hours there.

Voyage Tips and Advice

The cemetery map, which is accessible at the entry, will ensure that you do not miss any of the most magnificent structures.

B. The Leonardo Da Vinci Museum of Science and Technology

If you were wondering what to do in Milan for three days, the Leonardo da Vinci Museum of Science and Technology is a must-see.

To reach there from Monumental Cemetery, take the metro to Garibaldi station and then change lines to Ambrosio station. The museum is located only a few meters from Via San Vittore. The whole trip will take about 15-20 minutes.

If you want to walk from the cemetery, you can do so by passing via Arco della Pace and arriving at the museum in around 40 minutes.

The Leonardo da Vinci Museum of Science and Technology is massive and has several models inspired by the famous genius' ideas. It spans numerous levels and includes parts on aviation, rail and naval transportation, autos, space, and communications.

The museum welcomes children and provides an enjoyable family experience.

Admission to the museum is included in the Milan Pass, the Milan Digital Pass, or you may buy a skip-the-line ticket

Voyage Tips and Advice

Plan a half-day visit since there is so much to see. A minimum of three hours is required to finish the trip without loitering too long. Don't go just an hour before closing time.

C. The Basilica of St. Ambrogio

The Basilica of Sant'Ambrogio is within a three-minute walk from the museum.

This ancient landmark, known locally as Basicila di Sant'Ambrogio, is located next to a picturesque pedestrian street in a nice area. One of Milan's oldest cathedrals is named for the city's patron saint.

It is also regarded as a valuable symbol of Lombard Romanesque art. Although it was erected in 386, it has been demolished and rebuilt multiple times throughout the years.

This well-known church is distinguished by its two asymmetrical brick towers and unique architectural design. Inside, visitors may see superb goldsmith's work, Stilicho's sarcophagus, and a crypt containing the remains of various Italian saints, including the well-known Saint Ambrose.

The church's ceiling and nave are well worth seeing.

Voyage Tips and Advice

After seeing the Basilica of Sant'Ambrose, you can stroll 10 minutes to the church of Santa Maria delle Grazie in Milan, where one of the most exquisite paintings, "The Last Supper" by Leonardo da Vinci, is displayed.

Visits are, however, limited to certain days and hours and need a reservation. It's up to you to decide if it fits into your schedule. Tickets are on sale at getyourguide.com. (A Guided Tour of Da Vinci's Last Supper)

You can also go on a tour with a qualified guide, who will explain all you need to know about this wonderful painting.

Leonardo's Vineyard is located just next to the church. Tickets are on sale at @tiqets.com.

D. Navigli District

Next, on the second day of your 72-hour stay in Milan, I recommend taking a walk in the Navigli neighborhood.

This is Milan's most scenic neighborhood, as well as the heart of the city's nightlife. Aptly termed "the canal district," its success is owed to the network of canals that cross it and offer so much charm.

To get to the Navigli district from Saint Ambrose Church in 15 minutes, take Metro Line 2 from Ambrogio and get out at the Genova stop.

Then take your time walking down the canal, stopping for a drink or meal on a terrace, and finishing the evening in style at one of the area's restaurants, bars, or nightclubs.

The Navigli district is particularly lovely at the end of the day: stroll through its bustling streets under the beautiful light of the sunset!

Voyage Tips and Advice

Don't overlook Vicolo Lavandai on Alzaia Naviglio Grande. It's one of the nicest sites in the district and it's ideal for an evening walk while enjoying the festive atmosphere.

To explore the Navigli, nothing beats arranging a canal cruise with an aperitif. Visit tiqets.com for all the details.

Third day in Milan: Places to Visit

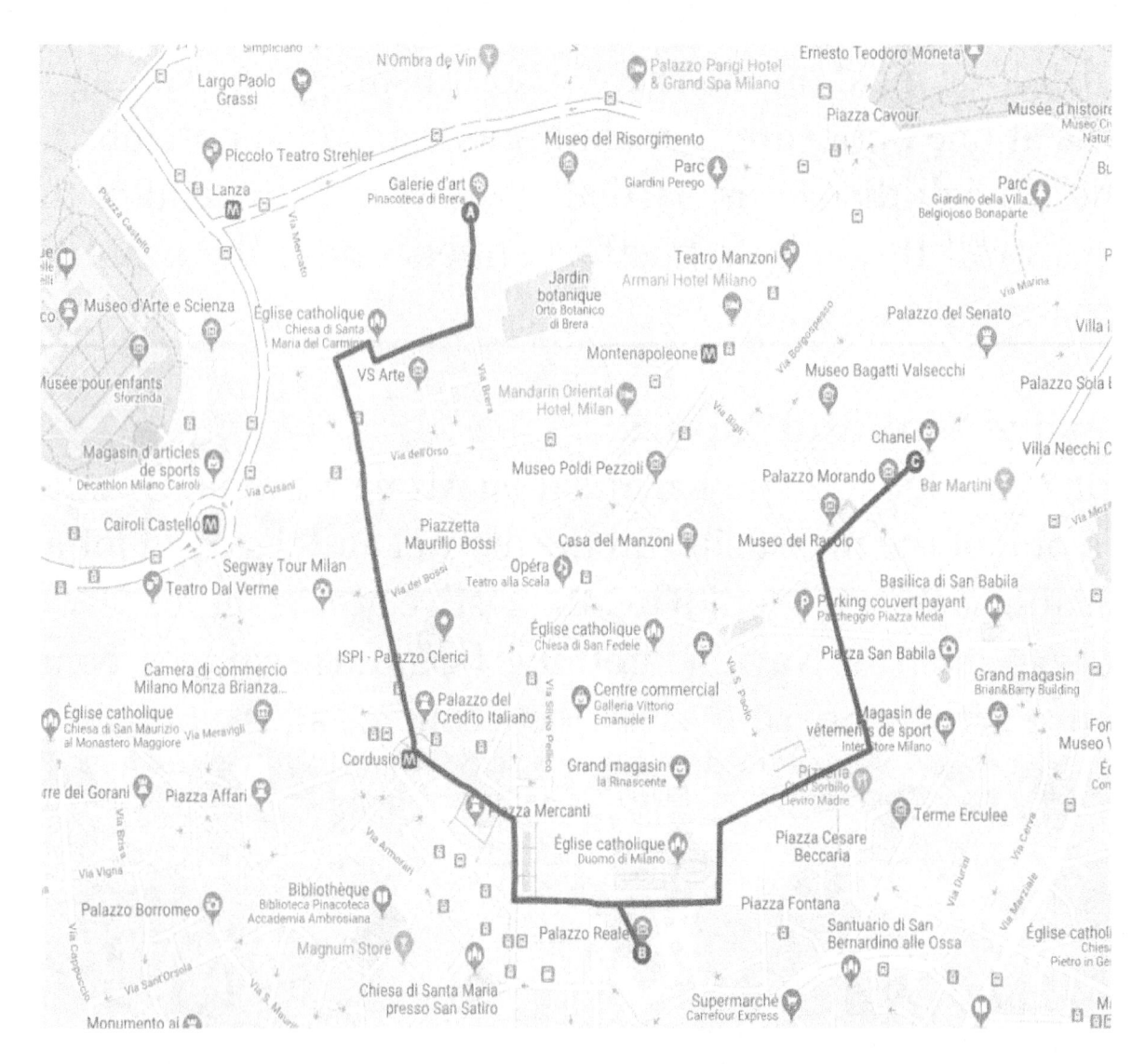

Day 3 visits

- A. The Pinacoteca
- B. The Royal Palace
- C. Shopping

A: Brera Pinacoteca

It's already the third and last day of your Milan schedule, but there's still plenty to see and do.

I recommend beginning with a visit to the Brera Art Gallery, the city's Fine Arts Museum. The Brera Pinacoteca, located within a 10-minute walk from Milan Cathedral, is one of Italy's most extensive art collections and is well worth the visit.

This gallery, housed in Palazzo Brera, used to be a monk cultural center. It also had a library and an astronomy observatory during the time.

This center's collection has evolved throughout the years, and the pieces on exhibit now comprise over forty rooms. Notably, you can see great paintings like Caravaggio's "The Supper at Emmaus" and Raphael's "The Marriage of the Virgin".

Expect to spend about 2 hours visiting.

B. The Royal Palace of Milan

Another iconic monument in Milan is the Royal Palace, which is located approximately a 15-minute walk south of the Pinacoteca.

To reach there, go down Via Brera to Piazza della Scala. To get to Milan Cathedral Square, go across the square and through the glass-roofed arcade. The palace is positioned right opposite the cathedral, to the left.

For many years, the Royal Palace of Milan served as the headquarters of the Milanese government, and it has subsequently become an important cultural center. Throughout the year, it presents art, fashion, and design exhibitions.

The Palace's museum showcases the city's history and residents. The Palace courtyard provides a stunning view of Milan Cathedral and is ideal for a walk.

On Mondays, the Palace is closed to the public. A visit costs 14€ at full price.

C. Shopping in Milan

How could you spend three days in Milan, the fashion capital, without going shopping?

I recommend concluding your time with a little window browsing in the city's commercial districts. The last day is ideal for making purchases and discovering unique things and souvenirs.

For those who want to indulge and celebrate the big Italian brands, I recommend walking along Via Montenapoleone, Via della Spiga, Via Sant'Andrea, and Via Manzoni. These four streets are home to a great number of fashion businesses and are around 15-20 minutes walk from the Palace.

Italian brands Gucci and Versace, among others, have boutiques here. This area also hosts the Milan Fashion Week.

For those on a tight budget, I recommend The Highline Outlet shopping gallery, which is about 5 minutes' walk from the cathedral square. You'll discover brands at reasonable pricing in a lovely setting.

D. Optional: San Siro Stadium and Casa Milan Museum

If you like football, you should visit San Siro Stadium and the Casa Milan Museum.

AC Milan followers will understand exactly what I mean! During the stadium guided tour, you may see the players' locker rooms and stands before continuing to the museum to see the trophy room and the Ballon d'Or hall.

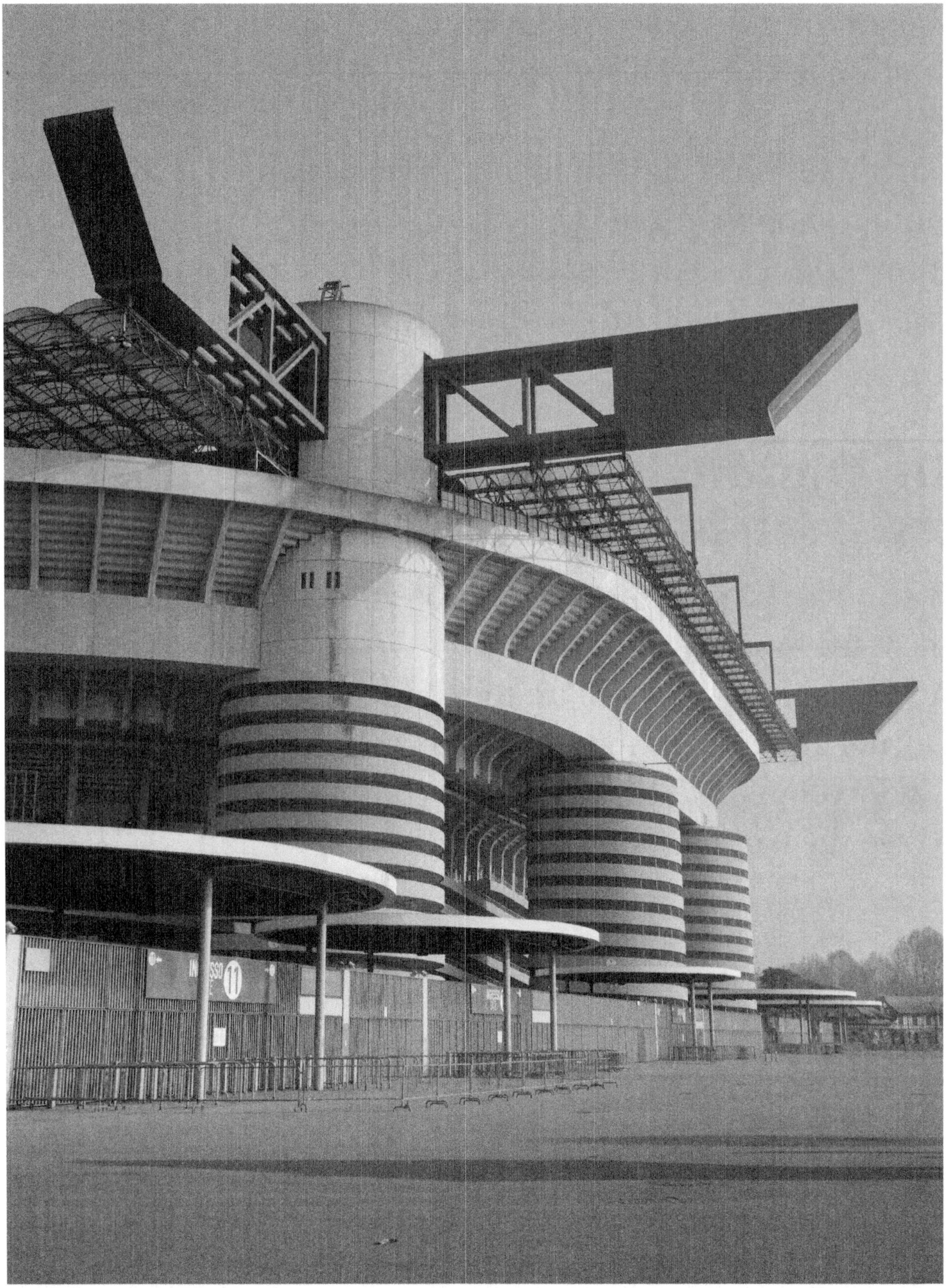
11

Where To Stay In Milan

Now that you know how to visit Milan in three days, let's talk about your accommodations: where will you stay?
So, here too, I make it simple for you with my pick of the top hotels to stay in Milan.

Ostello Bello Grande: Hostel near Milan Central Station. Dormitory beds start at 60 euros and include breakfast. Strong points: the greeting, the mood, and the cleanliness.

Hotel Da Vinci: Located just outside of the city center yet only a 10-minute walk from a metro station. Huge contemporary and light double rooms start at €90 per night, including breakfast. Strong points: quiet location, big rooms, free parking, and a generous buffet breakfast. This is my best choice for value for money!

43 Station Hotel: Located only steps away from Milan's central station. Modern and spacious rooms start at 130€ per night, including breakfast for 9€. Strong points: brand-new and well-equipped hotel, big breakfast, and excellent location.

Hotel Folen: Also near the station. Starting at 190€, you may have a spacious room with quality linen, including breakfast. Strong features include the location, the staff's kindness, and the full breakfast.

Rosa Grand Milano - Starhotels Collezione is a two-minute walk from the Duomo. Modern & attractive rooms, some with views of Milan Cathedral, start at 300€, including breakfast. Strong aspects include the central location in Milan, the wellness center, and friendly staff. A wonderful option for a luxurious stay in Milan!

Suite Milano Duomo is a 5-star hotel situated 5 minutes from the Milan Cathedral. Spacious and trendy rooms start at 325€/night. Location, hospitality, and personnel are its strong characteristics. It is my top suggestion for a romantic stay in Milan.

Visiting Milan in three days with family

If you want to visit Milan with your kids for three days, you can surely follow my day-by-day itinerary.

Even though the city is heavily focused on fashion, art, and culture, the majority of the activities are likely to appeal to people of all ages. Another benefit is the ease with which everything can be covered on foot. The majority of the attractions are close together, and the tour route is well-designed, so you will not have to go far.

Here's a short selection of family-friendly activities for three days in Milan.

The Leonardo da Vinci Museum is THE museum to see in Milan with your family. It is interesting and educative, allowing you to spend a pleasant and educational half-day immersed in the world of the legendary inventor's research and creations. The museum is extremely vast, so plan on spending 3 to 4 hours there. If you are hungry, there is a lunch place accessible on-site.

Milan Cathedral (Duomo): Impressive and a must-see, the city's symbol will fascinate children, teens, and people of all ages. Don't forget to climb up to the roofs for a breathtaking perspective of the city.

Sforza Castle: With its imposing look and architecture, children will be able to immerse themselves in the medieval atmosphere. The castle has many museums, where you might experience strange musical instruments, mummies, and sarcophagi. Don't miss the guided tour of the castle's underground.

The majestic San Siro Stadium often hosts prestigious teams such as AC Milan and Inter Milan. Perfect for aspiring players! Additionally, it is Italy's biggest stadium. Tickets are available at tiqets.com (Tickets for the San Siro Stadium Tour: Reserved Entrance

You might also want to consider visiting **The Natural History Museum** as a fun family activity on wet days. This museum dedicated to species evolution, wildlife, and flora is a fascinating option for spending quality time together. It is situated east of the city, a 4-minute metro trip from Duomo Square. Open from Tuesday to Sunday.

The Milan Aquarium is located near Sforza Castle. Every day after 4:30 p.m., entrance is free.

Triennale Kids is a museum for children aged 3 to 10, offering activities and games.

Idroscalo Park: Located somewhat outside of the city, this leisure area is ideal for family enjoyment. Plan on spending a good half-day or full day in the park, which is roughly an hour's drive from the city center.

Tickets for Leolandia amusement park, situated 40 minutes from Milan, are available at Tiqets.com. Super clean and well-kept, with lots of rides and exhibitions. A fantastic pick for a family day out in Milan!

Acquatica Park is a wonderful water park featuring pools, slides, and a paddling pool on the outskirts of Milan.

Acquaworld is another indoor and outdoor water park located around 20 kilometers from Milan.

BONUS

Travel Journal

Milan In 3 days

Date:
Location:
Budget:

DAY 1

Personal Itinerary

TODAY'S LOG

6 AM	
7 AM	
8 AM	
9 AM	
10 AM	
11 AM	
12 PM	
1 PM	
2 PM	
3 PM	
4 PM	
5 PM	
6 PM	

PLACES TO GO

REMINDER

39

Date:

Location:

Budget:

DAY 2

Personal Itinerary

TODAY'S LOG

- 6 AM
- 7 AM
- 8 AM
- 9 AM
- 10 AM
- 11 AM
- 12 PM
- 1 PM
- 2 PM
- 3 PM
- 4 PM
- 5 PM
- 6 PM

PLACES TO GO

REMINDER

Date:
Location:
Budget:

DAY 3

Personal Itinerary

TODAY'S LOG

- 6 AM
- 7 AM
- 8 AM
- 9 AM
- 10 AM
- 11 AM
- 12 PM
- 1 PM
- 2 PM
- 3 PM
- 4 PM
- 5 PM
- 6 PM

PLACES TO GO

REMINDER

Printed in Great Britain
by Amazon